DO THEY HAVE JOY IN THEIR HEART?

TIPS ON LIFE, LOVE AND THE PURSUIT OF HAPPINESS

ELAINE ORLAND

D1739122

ROSE GARDEN PRESS

DEDICATION

T his book is dedicated to each person mentioned in it. You will get to know them a little bit as well. A special shout out to patient hubby, Dave!

Cover art "Circles Aesthetic" and cover design by Angelee van Allman. Visit her website at angeleevanallman.com. She does many things, including custom and pre-made book covers; book interiors and formatting; illustrations and character design, and loads of other quirky stuff, and she is just darned fun. — Elaine

CONTENTS

Introduction   IX

1. Do They Wake Up Happy in the Morning?   1

2. Do They Use Turn Signals when Other Cars are in   2
   Sight?

3. Do They Speak Well of past Relationships?   4

4. Do They Tip Generously in Restaurants?   6

5. Do They Have a Spirituality that They Practice which   8
   Brings Them Peace?

6. Do They Have a Guiding Ideal?   10

7. When Something is Wrong or Broken, do They Try to   13
   Fix It Rather than Ignore It or Pass It on?

8. Do They Have a Sense of Humor?   15

9. Do They Easily Help Set Things Up and Clean Up   17
   Afterward?

10. Do They Not Take Things Personally Realizing that   19
    Not Everything Is About Them?

11. Are They Easy to Approach for Assistance or In Gen-   21
    eral?

12.	Can They Laugh at Themselves?	22
13.	Do They Help Out Without Being Asked?	23
14.	Can They Find the Positive in Any Situation?	25
15.	Do They Listen Carefully?	27
16.	Can They Admit when They Are Wrong?	29
17.	Do They Let Other Drivers Merge in Front of Them?	30
18.	Do They Enjoy Being Around Children?	32
19.	Do They Reach Out to Family and Friends and Keep in Touch?	33
20.	Do They Keep the Front Walk or Entryway Swept?	34
21.	Do They Experience Wonder in the Natural World?	35
22.	If They are Making Something, Do They Make Extra for Others...or at Least Share?	37
23.	If They Have an Addiction, Are They Living a Solid Recovery Lifestyle?	39
24.	Are They Kind and Personable to Wait-staff and People with Service Jobs?	41
25.	Are They Content with What They Have?	43
26.	Do They Make Their Bed when They Get Up?	45
27.	Do They Return the Shopping Cart to the Store or Official Cart Parking Place?	46
28.	Do They Forgive Easily?	48
29.	Do They Send Thank You Notes or Thoughtful Messages?	50
30.	Do They Laugh Easily?	52

31. Do They Try to Understand and Encourage Others and Never Tear Them Down?   53

32. Do They Smile Through Their Eyes?   55

33. Are They Patient and Compassionate When That is Called for?   56

34. Do They Sing, Whistle, Hum, or Dance Regularly?   57

35. Do They Volunteer Some of Their Time?   59

36. Do They Say "I Love You" to Friends?   60

37. Do They Give Compliments to Others?   61

38. Do They Take Care of Their Clothes: Sew on Buttons, Fix Hems, Hang Things Up?   63

39. Do They Seem to Know Things Will Turn Out All Right?   65

40. Do They Give to Charity Consistently?   67

41. Do They Make Direct and Kind Eye Contact?   69

42. Do They Seem to Like Themselves?   71

43. Do They Appreciate Pets?   73

44. Do They Follow Their Own Drum Beat?   74

45. Do They See Games and Competition as Fun Rather than as War?   75

46. Do They Have a Hobby that Engages Them or Sparks Their Creativity?   77

47. Are They Open and Easy Within Their Body?   79

48. Do They Still Do Some Fun Things They Liked as a Child?   81

49.	Do They Take Their Turn Doing Something Unpleasant, Like Chores?	82
50.	Do They Hang Around Other People with Joy in Their Heart?	84
In Conclusion		86
THE CHECKLIST		87
About Author		92

INTRODUCTION

One day, my sister-in-law, Lynn, several years post-divorce, was contemplating beginning the process of finding a new life partner. She said, "I want to find someone who has Joy in their heart." And that statement stuck with me. "Joy in their heart. Joy in their heart."

Why did that lodge itself in my mind? Was it important? I didn't know whether it was important or not to be around people who have Joy in their heart. I hadn't thought about it before. But here is what I began to imagine they could bring to a relationship. Fun! Magic! Spontaneity! Respect! Partnership! A sense of belonging! Love of life! Unconditional positive regard! The list went on...at least in my head it did.

Perhaps it was obvious why she would want someone with Joy in their heart, whatever that is, but how would she know? How would I? Ask them? That's not particularly reliable. Grill them? On what? "Maybe there are some indicators," thought I. So I went to work.

Being a therapist, I am quite familiar with people without Joy in their heart, at least at times. People with depression, sorrow, despair, confusion, questions. But Joy? I started looking around. It did not seem to be about the current life issue a person was working on; it was more about who they are as a person, their attitude, how they treat people and things, what is going on in their spirit. What is going on underneath.

Here is my working definition of Joy (especially Joy as contrasted with pleasure): picture a fireplace with a nice fire going. Logs on a grate, cracking and popping, yellow-orange flames licking up from the orange and black logs, and underneath, iridescent red-orange coals. The flames are what we notice the most. They are flashy! They come and go and change shape and eventually die down. Throw a wadded-up piece of paper on them and the flames will shoot up for a few seconds. That is similar to pleasure. It is great for a short space of time and moves on or dies down. Now, the collection of coals underneath . . . that is where the real power is. The fire can have died down and if you poke around on the coals, they have the power to start it up again with a little more fuel. The coals are like Joy. They are not flashy in the same way as the flames. They are hot and steady and have a great deal of potential stored in them and put off a consistent heat. Joy.

What you will read is an imperfect, subjective, and perhaps arbitrary list of "kernels of Joy" you might be able to detect. You may not agree with them all, you may have more to add--send them to me, (please!) --but I find they are a pretty good indicator of someone with Joy in their heart. Now, none of us has all of these. I have many deficits. But the more of these a person has, I think, a better chance it is that they have Joy in their heart.

You can start with the Checklist, and run a couple of your favorite, or not-favorite people through it. See how they rate. Some of the items are easy to spot. Some you may need to guess about. Then, at some point, you might want to put yourself through the checklist and see what your own Joy rating might be.

Here is my other theory. If I perceive myself to have a lack of Joy in my own heart, maybe I can reverse engineer some of the things on this list. Maybe I can begin to do some more of these things, and perhaps that seed of Joy might grow into a sprout, then a plant, then a tree raining fruits of Joy all around me! And wouldn't that be great? It's said that sometimes we can act ourselves into a new state of being. Perhaps working toward some of the things on this list might just increase our own level of Joy. It can't hurt to try!

You will note that many of the things listed are about being of service to others. There are plenty of sources that tell us that being of service to others is where our real Joy nut stash is, as well as a source of an increased sense of self-esteem and purpose.

Have fun with this list! A famous scientist once said that all models are flawed but some can still be useful. This might just be one of those models. I capitalize Joy to act as a little spark to activate a Joyful feeling in you when you see the word. Will that work? You tell me.

One caveat from daughter, Chelsea, after reading this is that some of what I suggest can be done from anxiety or from not wanting to be judged negatively. She is usually right.

-- Elaine Orland, November 2023

email: ElaineOrland57@gmail.com

ONE

DO THEY WAKE UP HAPPY IN THE MORNING?

M y spouse is amazing. No matter how rough the day or night before might have been, he wakes up in a good mood. At least that is what he shows to me. How does he do that? I am guessing there is some Joy in his heart. I do not claim to have Joy as abundant as that. Waking up happy seems like a glass-half-full way to start the day. Some people have practices that create this state of mind early in the day. Stretching, meditating, exercising, reading some inspirational literature, spending time with a pet, enjoying a warm beverage or a hot shower.

For me, it is often what has gone on the night before. Creating a reasonable bedtime so that I can get about eight hours of sleep (give or take an hour) makes a huge difference. That is sometimes hard to follow, especially when my phone is around, or a really diverting book of fiction. I sometimes have to wean myself off of electronic devices earlier in the evening to not get caught up in something "delicious."

What can or do *you* do to create Joy in your heart first thing in the day?

Two

DO THEY USE TURN SIGNALS WHEN OTHER CARS ARE IN SIGHT?

Having consideration for others seems to be an indicator of Joy. I lengthened this one from "Do they use turn signals," after my gym coach gave me a lot of "yeah buts" and "what abouts." I relented to the point of adding, "when other cars are in sight." It sometimes seems like a lost art, but to keep people guessing when we are driving several tons of explosive fluids and sharp glass and metal just does not add up to having Joy in the heart.

Husband Dave says he tries to use them even when there are not other cars around, "Just to keep in the habit." I am not so sure I am that virtuous, but I do know that I appreciate someone who uses them, and I judge them as being smarter, kinder, more gracious human beings. Is that wrong?

I believe Joy is more present when we are being considerate of others, not when we are upping the chances that we and they could crash and burn.

Besides, they make such a cute little clicking noise! And they tell me when they are burned out by clicking really fast. It took me a long time to figure out why they were doing that, but I'm a pretty smart cookie, and a glance through the manual let me know. These days the car manuals are probably online. Right.

Three

DO THEY SPEAK WELL OF PAST RELATIONSHIPS?

M ost of us have had relationships we would rather not remember and found ourselves entangled with someone to whom we just can't recall why we were attracted in the first place. But it is important to remember that we DID pick that person and that it is a very rare case when someone else forced us to link up with a partner. (At least in our society.) Still, when we have Joy in our heart, we also take responsibility for our decisions, healthy or not so healthy.

Finding something that is at least respectful to say of persons from our past is a sign of living in and accepting our reality. It often seems scrumptious to talk trash about someone with whom we are mad or have resentments. But that does not really do anything constructive about being mad or having resentments. Looking at our part, owning up to that, and learning from our patterns of behavior is part of growing up. I have heard it wisely said that I have not begun to think straight until I am able to find something in the lives of those I really dislike that I can truly admire. Hum . . .

It may take time, but if we have done our work, we can look for something positive to say about anyone we have known. If there is nothing positive to be found, then Joyful people generally will not say anything about them at all. Some of us are slow learners.

FOUR

DO THEY TIP GENEROUSLY IN RESTAURANTS?

S ome of you have worked in restaurants. It is a very tough job. On your feet for a whole shift, lifting heavy weights on slippery surfaces, putting up with unpleasant or absent co-workers and with customers who sometimes forget that a better part of your wages is from tips. (In some of those all-you-can-eat buffets, it might be the only wages.) We won't get into the politics and economics of this situation. The garlic green beans are just too tasty.

Granted, sometimes we can barely scrape together the dough to treat ourselves to eating out at all, and this is a condition almost all of us are in at various points in our lives. If that is the case, so be it. If we are in a more fortunate phase of our life, we might find that a Joyful heart wants to spread the love. This also means, on top of being a pleasant and swell customer, leaving a generous tip, so that the server can buy a decent brand of dog food for little four-footed Shnookums at home.

Of course, if picking up fast-food regularly is the lifestyle choice, then the tipping thing doesn't come into play, just the obesity, heart attacks, strokes, and diabetes. But, dang, that stuff is tasty!

FIVE

DO THEY HAVE A SPIRITUALITY THAT THEY PRACTICE WHICH BRINGS THEM PEACE?

S pirituality and spiritual or religious practice--very different things--come in more flavors than Baskin-Robbins ice cream, and I won't go into the details of any of them. I have just noticed that people with Joy in their heart generally have some sort of practice or philosophy or sense of a Higher Power, or of themselves being something deeper than meets the eye, that gives their experience of life more meaning, and also provides support and solace and sometimes guidance in times of trouble . . . or, actually, at any time.

Sometimes it takes a lot of looking around with an open mind to find some sort of spiritual or philosophical source that really resonates well inside. It can be quite a battle if we were raised with a very strong belief system. Sometimes there is a lot of unlearning to do first, or at least a willingness to entertain other possible perspectives.

Do they have a regular practice that tunes them in? Prayer, meditation, attentive listening, being in nature, service to others, Twelve-Step work, drumming, music . . . there are many paths up the mountain. Though we may seem separated by distance, creed, race or some other factor, we are all part of the same Whole.

I have an inner voice that I talk to that talks back, and no one has locked me up yet (but there is still time)! This practice brings me peace. Doing the exploration to find a spiritual perspective that really fits us well is a good use of our time and can bring us Joy throughout the rest of our life. It is a Joyful adventure and a good one for boosting the Joy-o-meter.

Six

DO THEY HAVE A GUIDING IDEAL?

W hat sort of life would I experience at home if everyone in it were just like me? What would my neighborhood or my workplace be like if every person there were just like me? So, what makes us behave like we do? There is a guiding ideal underneath it all. It is something that, whether we are aware of it consciously or not, influences everything we think, do, and feel. It pushes us toward who we eventually become. So, those are good questions to ask myself, and they are good observations to make in myself and others.

Do I have an ideal of "Joy" or "love" or "friendliness" or "peace" or "being helpful" or maybe if I look at myself, or another, I can sense an ideal of "disconnection" or "selfishness" or "fear" or "rebelling" or "wandering" or "revenge". How many of us would walk blindly into a restaurant we don't know, not knowing what sort of food they serve, refuse to look at a menu, and ask the wait-staff to "Just bring me anything." But, are we, maybe, doing that with life?

It is important to get conscious of my guiding ideal, and to adjust it if it needs adjusting or changing. Why? Because it uses my energy and shapes my life. It gives me a push, direction and guidance, when choices show up in my life. When I do what I know to do, how to BE, because of my ideal then the next step seems to come along more readily. As I achieve my stated ideal (by all means, write it down!), my ideals for myself can grow deeper over time. It is like creating a painting; it can be worked on carefully over time until it is something we can proudly share.

Perhaps getting conscious of mine might make it easier for me to guess at the guiding ideal or ideals in someone else.

So, what WOULD my (relationship, home, place of worship, workplace, neighborhood — you pick it) be like if everyone in it was just like me? Just what do I have in MY heart?

SEVEN

WHEN SOMETHING IS WRONG OR BROKEN, DO THEY TRY TO FIX IT RATHER THAN IGNORE IT OR PASS IT ON?

F rankly, I do not know if this one is just built into some of us or if it has to be taught, but there is a mindset that some people have of seeing something that has a problem or needs fixing, and they start right in on taking care of it, either on their own or by arranging for assistance. "Git 'er done" is how we say it down South.

There is another mindset that thinks that entropy, break down, is just what happens and that the best thing to do is pretend like it doesn't matter or that someone else will take care of it.

And maybe there is a third perspective that is out there where something broken or amiss is just not noticed at all, at least not enough to register. I am thinking that the person with Joy in their heart wants things to be in good running order, but I could be wrong on this one.

Maybe it is more Joyous to be clueless. I'm not sure. Let me know what you think.

EIGHT

DO THEY HAVE A
SENSE OF HUMOR?

I am not sure that this one even needs explaining, but Joy and humor are bedfellows. They get all up in each other's face. It takes a great deal of humor for us, in our fallible state, to stay Joyous in this world. We often do things wrong and regularly see tragic things, and finding something light about those things is what humor is all about.

Think of almost any joke. It is likely to be based on something tragic . . . or at least something tough. "How do you get down off an elephant?" "You don't get down off an elephant, you get down off a duck." It is a play on the word "down," but the poor duck is still getting it in the end.

If it is used to lighten the tragic (while, of course, honoring others' pain and feelings) then, good deal. However, humor can also deflect legitimate feelings or attention from something painful, or from a confrontation that we, perhaps, should pay more attention to, even if it is uncomfortable. Sometimes we just need to step up to the plate and face the music (insert your own cliche here). But providing that we are not using it to hide from reality, humor is the quickest remedy to move from a negative state of mind to one of Joy, or at least to a brighter outlook. It is also at the top of my list of attributes for a good friend.

NINE

DO THEY EASILY HELP SET THINGS UP AND CLEAN UP AFTERWARD?

There is a well-kept secret that one of the quickest ways to be accepted, feel at home, and draw friendly energy to yourself (thus raising your self-concept) is to jump right in there and help set stuff up. At a meeting or gathering, set up chairs, make coffee, sweep up crumbs, wipe down tables, ask how to be helpful. And afterward, reverse that: put away chairs, clean up the coffee . . . okay, you can still sweep up crumbs and wipe down tables. People will assume you feel comfortable and treat you like you are somebody. You will begin to feel like you are somebody, and that little Joy Place near your heart will start to glow a bit. This can become a habit because people discover that it is a good way to increase inner Joy, and who can't use more of that?

I am somewhere right in the middle of the introverted / extroverted scale. I tend to be more introverted around new people or places. I am not very good at small talk and chitchat. I lost that skill along the way.

So, I began the practice of jumping in there, fear and all, to be helpful whenever possible, and so now most people think I am an extroverted, can-do person. I guess I am a sheep in wolf's clothing. "Bah-h-h-h grrrrrrooowwwll."

Ten

DO THEY NOT TAKE THINGS PERSONALLY REALIZING THAT NOT EVERYTHING IS ABOUT THEM?

I can have a sense of being-a-part-of, or of me-against-the-world. A cooperative, joining, attitude allows me to give and take, to learn and teach, to be a-part-of. Taking things personally shows a self-turned focus. It is all about me. You are all about me. This is a normal state for a child. In that developmental state, so much must be learned from a very early age until becoming grown that self-focus is appropriate and allows a little one to be a learning sponge.

When I view everything as a reflection of me or an afront to me as an older person, I am living out of a younger ego state. Something in me has just gotten stuck; not grown up yet. To remedy this, I generally need some assistance from a therapist, Twelve-Step sponsor, pastor or other helping professional, or a super-wise friend, to break through that stuck-ness and realize that, "It just ain't all about me. Sometimes it is about something that has nothing to do with me. I just happened to be in the target zone."

I have a little trick I do when I find someone really annoying to me. Humor, in this, like many things, can help. I think, "If they were a cartoon character, which one would they be?" Generally, when I can see them in this way, their repeating behaviors become expected, in character, and often quite funny.

ELEVEN

ARE THEY EASY TO APPROACH FOR ASSISTANCE OR IN GENERAL?

O kay: granted, for many of us it is not easy to ask for help from anyone. We have been taught that it is weakness to need help, to not be able or have the knowledge to do something ourselves, blah, blah, blah. And some people are, in fact, formidable to approach. They may have energy that can back us off.

However, if they have Joy in their heart, they seem to move forward to meet us in our approach. Or better yet, they will often make the approach to us if they sense we are in need. Even if that might feel uncomfortable... just because . . . It also can be a Godsend and help us get over the asking hump.

People with Joy in their heart are eager to be of help when they see the need. Something about, "When you help someone else, it helps you, too." Or maybe they have just realized the principle that being of service is the quickest way to creating Joy (or alleviating anxiety, as daughter Chelsea might say).

TWELVE

CAN THEY LAUGH AT THEMSELVES?

We are the silliest and most fallible critters, we humans. Our bodies are soft, easy to injure, and prone to accidents. I mean, look at all those long dangly appendages sticking out of our trunks. We can do a bunch of things, but gosh, we are vulnerable.

And then there's that bunchy gray blob in our head. We have very little idea what that chunky mass is really good for. But one thing that it sometimes does is tell us things that are just not true, or it has us doing things that are not in our own or anyone else's best interest. Sometimes it has us just not coordinating our various thinking and doing parts very well and the result is something weird coming from our body or our mouth or our mind.

We are just generally goofy, and folks who take themselves too seriously run the risk of having little Joy in their heart. Laughing at myself both releases tension in me and can diffuse an uncomfortable situation. This is often a good use of humor. It also hits the restart button and lets us take a different tack.

Thirteen

DO THEY HELP OUT WITHOUT BEING ASKED?

This one is perhaps similar to the one about helping to set up and clean up, just a little wider in focus. People with Joy in their heart seem to have enough outward focus to see a bigger picture of what needs to be done in many situations. They value being there for their fellow life travelers and do not see giving of their energy as depleting their own stock. They see the available alchemy of turning dross into gold: something seemingly not pleasant into something that provides treasure.

Because of this, they tend to be volunteers. Their hands go up early. There is a caution for our well-meaning ones, however. Overextending is a real hazard, and helpfulness and enabling are close cousins. The tricky bit is to check out what might be the motive behind the action. Am I doing it because someone has requested it and I know the Joy created by pitching in and helping, or because I think I have to, or want to be noticed, or, "Cuz no-danged-body-else is going to do it." If so, I need to stop and take a beat and change my perspective before proceeding so that I can leverage the Joy-creating capacity, leave it alone, or know I am going to have a resentment to work through later.

FOURTEEN

CAN THEY FIND THE POSITIVE IN ANY SITUATION?

Where does this come from, this "Pollyanna" way of viewing the world? By the way, being called a "Pollyanna" came from Eleanor H. Porter's 1913 novel about an overly optimistic orphan of the same name. It is supposed to be a put-down, like saying someone is out of touch with the seriousness of the world, but I have always taken it as a delightful compliment. It is kind of like being a glass-half-full person. And that expression came from seeing a partially filled glass as half-empty or as half-full. Same glass, same amount of liquid . . . different perception. Or how about "every cloud has a silver lining."

Enough of the old phrases for positive perspectives. You get the idea. When we have Joy in our heart, though we may feel sadness or sorrow, or know there can be a dire situation, we also know that there is always a little brightness in the dark if we look for it. A little space for faith.

An attitude of openness and trust is a sliver of faith; an aware-ness inside, sparked by something deeper that allows energy to work through us in spite of our imperfections, or our problems. An aware-ness of our wholeness. It is not a thing, it is a force of the soul and it is exercised through doing things for others. Finding and sharing that brightness lessens the dark. You can lighten a dark room with one little match. And the lightness on the end of the match or lighter comes from friction. We can perform some of that alchemy. That faith in action results in virtue and understanding . . . the practical application of knowledge we get from our experiences.

So, maybe it is not just *finding* the positive in a situation, but *creating* the positive. Do they do that?

FIFTEEN

DO THEY LISTEN CAREFULLY?

I have to catch myself with this one. Often, when someone is talking, I will be thinking of what I want to say back that sounds wise, or clever, or lets them know I am hip or cool (which by using those two terms right there let you know I probably am neither).

There is a sense in many of us that we need to perform in a conversation, when the reality is that if we listen with our soul to another person, really listen, we will find the right response when it is the right time . . . even if that response is to just be quiet and be with them.

A person with Joy in their heart may realize they do not know what to say back or that they need some time to think and process what has been said. They can say, "I need some time to think about that. I will get back to you." My mother taught me how to respond to someone sharing about a tough situation in their life when I had nothing brilliant to offer. She used to just say, "That seems hard." I have found this to be helpful personally and professionally.

Speaking of Mom: the other response she taught me was for those times when I did not want to comment to what I have heard with, "Are you out of your ever-lovin' mind!?" She would just say, "That's interesting." That way I was not agreeing, disagreeing, condoning, or resisting what had been said. I was just letting the other person know that I had heard them.

Sixteen

CAN THEY ADMIT WHEN THEY ARE WRONG?

To me, this is one of the clearest indicators of a person's level of self-esteem, and in this case, Joy. Can a person readily admit to their faults or mistakes when it becomes apparent? I have heard so many tales from people who say their father, or sometimes their mother, could never own up to their mistakes. What that does is show that that person is trying to wear a God-suit, be infallible. That just doesn't happen in the real world. A person with Joy in their heart can claim responsibility for their actions even when they are embarrassing, and often can find humor in the situation. Then they do what they can to make it right. If they have a shame attack from realizing they have really made an ass of themselves, they have ways to work through that...generally with a support person who can walk them back into feeling okay again. Some believe that a strong person doesn't admit to mistakes, but I find that is only true in prison, whether an actual jail or prison, or a prison of the mind. A strong person can see themselves realistically, take responsibility for their actions, and make amends and corrections as needed . . . coming back to Joy.

SEVENTEEN

DO THEY LET OTHER DRIVERS MERGE IN FRONT OF THEM?

"My bumper is farther forward than yours."

"How dare you come into my lane?"

"I was here first."

"Let me in, you jerk!"

"No way, don't you think you are better than me." "There, I did it! I am victorious and you are a loser!"

Sound familiar? It sometimes does in my brain, but I really try to practice in this situation. "Just let them go first." That is what I say to myself. Actually, I give them a little blessing at the same time. The effect of this is that I don't think about it for very long afterward. I am on with my day's adventure. If I have a little mental or automobile jousting match, it can color my day in a negative way. It is just not worth it.

Actually, that blessing thing comes in handy in the car a lot. At a particularly long red light, or traffic slowdown, I often will look at the people in each car and bless each one I can see. I figure it can't hurt, and maybe it can bring in a bit more Joy in their lives. The trick in blessing is to try to first work up in yourself the feeling you want to give to another, be it Joy or peace or whatever you choose. Then just say something like, "Bless you!" or "I give you peace." or "Joy to you!" I have found that even if I can't work that feeling up in myself at first, after I do a dozen or so blessings, I am feeling much more Joyful or peaceful than I was when I started. It is a win-win.

Eighteen

DO THEY ENJOY BEING AROUND CHILDREN?

People with Joy in their heart tend to be curious people. They are interested in things other than themselves and their own needs. They have found a store of energy that they can share with others, and often they find the innocence and authenticity of children fulfilling to be around.

One thing that attracted me to the man who became my husband was how I saw him interacting with his little nieces and nephews. He would get onto the floor with them and talk with them or play with them like they were honest-to-gosh valuable and interesting people. It is astounding to watch people do this, and for some of them, it is the most natural thing in the world. Amazing. Me? I do this better with cats.

People with Joy in their heart enjoy the spontaneity of the behavior of children. They can roll with it. They are not threatened by it. They tend to make good parents.

Nineteen

DO THEY REACH OUT TO FAMILY AND FRIENDS AND KEEP IN TOUCH?

Sometimes when I am writing these, I wish I could claim "YES! I do that!" But sometimes I don't. I listen to my husband talking to his elderly mother and father on the phone several times a week, and I think about my aunts and cousins and old friends. However, I still believe an indicator of Joy in your heart is that consistent effort to check on loved ones new and old. As the song goes, "Make new friends, but keep the old; one is silver and the other gold." There is wisdom in that. A phone call, text, note card, anything. It is worth it for the level of stability it can provide as well as for weaving one's roots together to make a stronger base.

My millennial daughter, Chelsea, says that this is often done in her peer group by sending GIFs or other small tech bits to loved ones. She says this lets them know you get who they are and are thinking about them. I don't doubt this. I say, whatever works!

TWENTY

DO THEY KEEP THE FRONT WALK OR ENTRYWAY SWEPT?

"What?! What could that possibly have to do with Joy in one's heart? Sounds like work to me." Ah, yes, it can be work . . . but not much of it. What it signifies is that people are welcome, looked out for, and cared about. Even if that person is you when you walk into your own home. My mom taught me this one. She said that it shows that you have prepared for their visit. I got myself a short, light, wispy broom from the local Asian market and I find I look forward to using it and making leaves dance in the air with it. Whoosh-whoosh.

Okay, true confessions: I also have two blowers, which are fun in their own way, but don't give me the satisfaction or the feel of creating a welcome as the light broom. Perhaps part of it is that I get to see each leaf when I am using the broom versus blasting their tiny little dry bodies away with the blowers. The blowers do, however, give me the satisfaction of dealing with larger spaces. Clears them right up!

TWENTY-ONE

DO THEY EXPERIENCE WONDER IN THE NATURAL WORLD?

There is Joy popping out all over. No matter the season. It is winter here right now, and I just lost myself for minutes of delight watching two squirrels chase each other in the bare trees in the back yard. Ahh. I get the same sense of wonder when buds pop out, leaves turn colors, fruits and vegetables grow, rivers flow, or when I sense the other beings that just might be living near us, seen or unseen. Again, mom: she said, "You don't know what sort of being might be right there with you, just vibrating at a rate that our eyes can't see, like those mosquitoes in Africa. They bounce up and down on their legs so quickly that they are invisible to us." Or maybe it was flies.

At any rate, there is our inside ecology, our outside ecology, and probably at least one more whole world of incredible diversity out there for those with eyes to see and ears to hear. Open up to the available Joy that can come from a walk around the block. Our daughter

just told me she saw ten deer yesterday on the property behind ours.
Zowie.

TWENTY-TWO

IF THEY ARE MAKING SOMETHING, DO THEY MAKE EXTRA FOR OTHERS...OR AT LEAST SHARE?

"That's mine . . . and . . . that's mine . . . and . . . oh yeah, that one is for sure mine." Sound familiar? It does to me, especially around food. Being a food addict, I do not share food well without a lot of warning. I do better in other areas, or when someone holds my hand, looks deeply into my eyes, and *then* says, "Would you mind if I have one of your French fries?" Each of us can have areas where sharing is difficult.

Carlos is a client of mine. He has recently come out of jail and is just pleasant to be around. Not long ago I warned him to watch out for the snacks he had brought to group with him or they might disappear, as does anything edible brought to group therapy. Carlos, who has very little of anything of his own, said, "Oh, I don't mind. I'm always willing to share." That rather stopped me in my tracks. He made the Joy list.

A person with Joy in their heart probably already knows who is around, and what those people like, and have planned on that when they make whatever it is they are making. There is a generosity about them that knows that they will be taken care of, that there is plenty to go around. They do not share my begrudging attitude . . . well, unless they are addicted to something as well. Which brings us to . . .

TWENTY-THREE

IF THEY HAVE AN ADDICTION, ARE THEY LIVING A SOLID RECOVERY LIFESTYLE?

W e are not going to ex out everyone with an addiction, because, frankly, there would be very few people left on the Joy list, BUT . . . if they have had their struggles with addiction, are they working some sort of recovery program, Twelve-Step or otherwise, that encourages, supports, and educates them and others? And do they offer up all those things for others who share their addiction? There are hundreds of different "anonymous" programs now, according to the World Service Office of Alcoholics Anonymous. It seems that if I have a problem with something and I am ready to get better, there is a group which has a solution for me. Besides those programs, often there are people that have put together groups or programs or therapy groups or spiritual groups or counselors who can help point someone with some honesty, open-mindedness, and willingness down a good path. Just Google it! That is an excellent path to creating Joy and to healing our planet.

Twenty-Four

Are They Kind and Personable to Wait-Staff and People with Service Jobs?

Think of it as a recon mission whenever you are with someone at a restaurant, or a store, for that matter. Check out your new friend and see how they treat the person behind the counter or taking their order or sweeping the bathroom they just used (well, maybe you won't be in there for that). But you get the idea. Do they treat them like valuable people or like levers in the gimme-what-I-want machine?

Do they know that we all share a common bond – are all in community with each other? Do they know that we have a pattern of wholeness which moves us in search of fulfillment, service and love for one another? Do they show warm regard (the minimum requirement of respect) to others; connect how they can and hold up their end of a relationship, no matter how brief?

My friend Rubydel is a master at this. She can turn anyone who crosses her path into a fast friend. It just takes a question or two, some direct eye contact, and good listening skills (all talked about in this book), and in her case, a heavy southern accent (which is not mandatory). She is a M-A-S-T-E-R. And she has Joy in her heart, for sure. Hers has not been a perfect life, but, shoot, she took up ballroom dancing once and ended up building a studio in her hometown so she could practice, share her passion with others, and hire great teachers. She lost weight, won trophies, got all graceful, and got to wear sparkly clothes, all at the same time! I think she even got married out of the deal, but that is her story to tell. Look for your own Rubydels.

TWENTY-FIVE

ARE THEY CONTENT WITH WHAT THEY HAVE?

The trick to having what you love is to love what you have. When I look back on places that husband Dave and I have lived, I am dumbfounded. We went from a one-bedroom apartment in a walk up to a single-wide house trailer in the country to a small two-bedroom home to the house across the street from that one (which had been my mother's), with four bedrooms and a mother-in-law suite.

At each of these places, we were able to manage with the amount of space and storage we had. And at each of these places, every nook and cranny got filled up with things I couldn't possibly get rid of . . . What *is* that? I think it would be interesting to go back to a living space the size of a house trailer and see what we would keep of our accumulated stuff.

Anyway, a wise man once said that the main problem in the world is not greed, it is envy. That made me think, because I sure thought it was greed. But maybe there is something to that, that we keep wanting things other people have rather than loving what we have. I think that beautiful or quirky or delightful things just like to follow me home and then I have to find a place for them. I know they are there, and I wait.

Some people equate patience with being passive or submissive, but it is neither. It is active . . . an active state of being aware of all the influences in a situation, and being open and receptive to right timing and right expression of the Soul. It is love in action. It brings Joyousness in everyday activities.

One time I took a challenge to cut down my wardrobe (including clothes, coats, shoes, and accessories) to thirty-three things per season. Period. Oh, not counting pajamas, underwear or gym clothes providing you only wear them to the gym. I did it! I gave away a mountain of clothes. So how did my closet get crammed full again? Enough is enough...clear out the space, make room for Joy!

Twenty-Six

Do They Make Their Bed When They Get Up?

I confess, I rate a big "No" on this one. I am not happy about that, but that unhappiness does not, as of this writing, outweigh my drive to move into my generally overcrowded day. However, I think that making the bed each morning is one of the easier ways of shifting the early morning (or whenever your morning is) into a place of Joy. It is just pleasant to see a smooth bed with a pillow or two or eight, ready to provide a place of rest at the end of the day (or naptime for some of us). So, will I pledge to pop up every morning and make our bed? Nah, not a pledge, but I will think about it more.

My sister, Rachel, says this one is not going to fly with younger generations, and that might be so. It didn't seem to fly with me, but I still believe there is a psychological boost that comes from seeing a put-together bed. There are catalogs full of them! But it might just be worth trying for a time, to see if it makes any psychological difference.

TWENTY-SEVEN

DO THEY RETURN THE SHOPPING CART TO THE STORE OR OFFICIAL CART PARKING PLACE?

We all think about it. If we aren't wheeling the grocery cart all the way home--please don't--there is the question as soon as the contents of the cart are unloaded into the car: "Where am I going to put the cart?" At many stores there is a designated spot, an official rack or two in the parking lot. I try to park near one of these. But the real test is: what about the parking lot that has no remote cart racks?

"The car is unlocked; do I leave it?"

"Do I really want to walk it all the way back to the store?"

"Could I just leave it on the parking space lines, or on that little piece of grassy mulch stuff?"

"Isn't it someone's job to collect these things?"

"Why don't they have any darned racks out here?"

And on and on. The truth is that by the time I go through the debate in my head, I could have walked the cart back inside the store.

Yes. I said inside the store, not just to the sidewalk in front where it could roll off and damage someone's car. So, I decided long ago to just walk them back to the inside of the store, and sometimes I get a hearty "Thank you!" from the store clerk. One little Joy point! Ka-ching!

TWENTY-EIGHT

DO THEY FORGIVE EASILY?

F ace it. Sometimes people do things that hurt us. Sometimes it hurts for a long time. Sometimes we think we are giving them what they deserve by not forgiving them. Sometimes we are wrong. So, let's be clear. Forgiveness is never for the other person. Forgiveness is always for us. "What!? Even if they are a jerk!?" Until we forgive another person, they have us by the short hairs. They own us, or at least part of us.

So, how can we think about forgiveness in another way? Forgiveness is not about saying that what they have done is okay with us or that we condone it. Often it is way not okay. However, forgiveness is about saying, "I am not going to give this thing power over me anymore. I am going to let it go." Face it, half the time, whoever did something to us either doesn't remember it, remembers it differently, or is gone. Often it only lives in us. There are no thought police making sure everyone remembers everything just like we do.

We all have patterns that are burdensome, that we wish we didn't have, that seem to shut out the light. This is time for self-forgiveness. Over time, we learn from both our "mistakes" as well as our "successes".

Maybe more so from our mistakes. If we can see them as teaching tools, and growth producers, maybe we can learn and let go more quickly. We have the chance to see each lesson as an opportunity for soul growth.

Forgiveness is about taking back our power, often power that we have handed over to the person we least want to have power over us. Forgiveness is about self-love, self-empowerment, and freedom. A person with Joy in their heart has learned this and forgives as quickly as possible.

Twenty-Nine

DO THEY SEND THANK YOU NOTES OR THOUGHTFUL MESSAGES?

D o They Send Thank You Notes or Thoughtful Messages?

Ah, we have hit upon one of my own superpowers. Now, a disclaimer: I have had several people say that this is another one that does not wash with younger generations . . . but it is still a superpower. Note writing . . . the lost art of note writing. Okay, its cousins, the text and email can be pretty good, too, but nothing packs a punch like a nice handwritten note or thank you card. (Our son-in-law, Joe, disagrees. He is a millennial and detests anything on paper. Just ask him.) But you just ask your grandmother, or any grandmother.

Just today, we were having a party at work. I had set up a wee holiday party for my clients. These are people with severe mental illness coming out of jail. Many from very tough lives. I put out the usual suspects: cookies, snack cakes, candy, ornaments, cute napkins and plates. I had a stack of holiday cards in my hand in which I had written something personal and special about each of them. I said I had one for each of them. One of the clients said, "A personal note for each of us?!?" They seemed to like those more than anything else in front of them. After the party there was plenty of trash left on the tables, but only one card . . . and that fellow's eyesight keeps him from being able to read, so I will read it to him when he comes back. Note cards . . . so easy to do.

There are two women I know, Bonnie and Chip, who send the most delightful cards which they embellish with stickers and markers and drawings. Such a big bang for your buck. One of my party fellows even said, "I really needed to read that today." Joy.

THIRTY

DO THEY LAUGH EASILY?

I have to talk about my friend Deborah here. If you were going to picture Mrs. Santa Claus, you would get a pretty good picture of Deborah. Maybe Mrs. C. with strawberry blonde hair. Her face is almost always lit up with a smile, she is ready for a hug, and she is primed and ready to laugh. When she laughs, your whole body vibrates. No, I don't think it is your body, it is your soul. She has an infectious laugh that gives the impression of bells ringing. Now it is not that Deborah doesn't have bad days; she does. She tells me about them. But pretty soon she is back to laughing and my soul is back to feeling vibrations of Joy. Sometimes I talk to her to experience her joie de vivre as well as to listen to her wisdom. She has plenty of both and is willing to share.

People who laugh seem to experience an "open-door" way of being. They live so that the light of their lives provides hope and encouragement to others.

My dentist, Dr. Mark, is another person for whom laughing comes easily. It has kept me going to his office and had made the trips to the dentist less daunting. Well, that and gas.

THIRTY-ONE

DO THEY TRY TO UNDERSTAND AND ENCOURAGE OTHERS AND NEVER TEAR THEM DOWN?

My astonishing Coach, John, gave me this one. I was lifting barbells as I am wont to do a couple of days a week, and I was fishing for some ideas about people having Joy in their heart. He thought about it for a while, attending to lifters' needs in his caring, respectful, delighted-to-work-with-you way and he came back to me and said, "They encourage people and don't EVER put them down." He pointed...pointedly with his pointer finger on that EVER, and you know, I have never heard him put anyone down. Not EVER. This is a guy that I watched a full year to try to determine if he could really be that nice, encouraging, wellspring of support I saw or if the mask would eventually slip. I finally determined that it was not faked. Not a put-on. How that bundle of Joy does it is still a mystery, but he just lights up a room, or a gym in this case.

When I experience this, it makes me want to follow suit. I want to be like that. I know his life is not pain-free. There are just as many trials there as for anyone, but that does not color the tone of his actions and words toward others. Amazing. His businesses seem to do well, too. I am guessing these things are connected.

Thirty-Two

DO THEY SMILE THROUGH THEIR EYES?

There is something about a smile that comes through the eyes. The mouth is involved, of course, and all those muscles around the chin and cheeks and lips and all. Good stuff. But real smiles move all the way up the face. There is a sparkle, a crinkle, a wee opening of the window into the soul. When that window opens, there is an energy rush that can flow out and knock your socks off. We have all seen those smiles.

Our son-in-law, Joe, has that kind of smile. I am certain that some marriages have taken place because of one of those. Maybe that is why Joe is our son-in-law. Perhaps that has happened even in my own history. So, take it from one who knows, be cautious around those Joy-filled smiles. They can make you weak in the knees and make you break out in weddings. But then, maybe that is the kind of Joy you are looking for!

Thirty-Three

ARE THEY PATIENT AND COMPASSIONATE WHEN THAT IS CALLED FOR?

I've got to go back to hubby, Dave, on this one, BECAUSE, I am not particularly patient and often not nearly as compassionate as I wish I was. Dave is pretty good at these. I watch him with kids (mentioned before; how it snagged this gal as a life partner) and with elders and I am envious. My mind is usually running 90-to-Nothing, or I am trying to think of the next thing to say or do and I miss out on this opportunity for service. (And did I say yet that he STILL sends snail-mail birthday cards?!)

People who can extend themselves like that may not be thinking about it, but I think about it when I see them . . . that what is healing for one, helps heal all. And healing and Joy are somehow connected. That's my story and I'm sticking to it!

THIRTY-FOUR

DO THEY SING, WHISTLE, HUM, OR DANCE REGULARLY?

I have taken up tap dancing again. It is delightful. I bought myself some tap shoes online (buy them at least a size larger than your street shoes--they run small), got a tabletop on sale at IKEA (to preserve our wooden floors) and bought a buncha lessons from United Tap online--Rod dishes out Joy with every guided step--and I tap-tap-tap on my tabletop on the floor until I have gone through a full glass of water. Am I any good? Certainly not! Do I have fun? Oh, yes I do . . . and my heart gets a good workout as well. When I am not tapping, you can generally find me singing or writing songs for a theater troupe created to perform at events geared toward people in recovery from various addictions. Recovery Repertory Theatre we are called, and we have an amateurish blast . . . and perhaps spread a little hope at the same time.

I used to work at a children's home run by a Catholic order of sisters. Once a week, Father David would come by to celebrate mass and talk with some of the children. From my office I could hear the door from the parking lot open and a bright and cheery whistle down the hall. I knew, "Father David is in the building," and it was going to be a good day. He spread Joy like nobody's business!

Practicing creative expression and keeping a song in your heart seems to me to come from Joy, or maybe it just creates it! What do you think?

Thirty-Five

DO THEY VOLUNTEER SOME OF THEIR TIME?

"I ain't doin' nothin' if I ain't getting' paid."

I don't know how many times I have heard that from people I work with who don't have a pot to piss in. This eyes-turned-inward self-focus is guaranteed to reduce the opportunities to experience Joy. The perspective that you've got to give something to get some back just doesn't sink in, and they will probably always experience lack.

Giving to others in some area where we can, creates an energy flow that comes back to us. The more we give, the more we receive. Now that doesn't mean giving until you are hurting yourself. That is codependency and needs a good recovery program. But giving of self opens doors, makes connections, brings unexpected gifts from the Universe. It takes the focus off me-me-me, which is myopic and stifling, and allows our Joy to blossom as we have a chance to be helpful.

There was a bumper sticker some decades back that said, "Practice random acts of kindness and senseless acts of beauty." I was just looking up the wording of this old bumper sticker and saw that there are websites dedicated to this practice. I know what I will be reading later this week, getting my Joy meter jumping.

Thirty-Six

DO THEY SAY "I LOVE YOU" TO FRIENDS?

There is a special feeling when we hear, "I love you." Or the more hedging, "I love ya, man." From a friend. It pushes against some internal mores that tell us "They'll misunderstand." "What if they think I am coming on to them?" "Is it really love that I feel? Do I know them that well?"

No matter. People with Joy in their heart let those they love know that they love them. Easy-peasy. It might feel awkward the first time, but it gets easier thereafter and adds a layer of confidence to the connection. I have quite a few friends in various Twelve-Step communities, and that is a place I have used to verbally spread "I love you" around. It seems appreciated, and I like to hear it as well. Maybe its meaning is more like, "I really like you a lot." But maybe there is a deeper connection that "I love you" honors. And that is something we can all use more of . . . confidence in our connections. When you feel it, see if you can catch the Joy in a casual "I love you" or, yes, "Love ya, gal!" and see how it sits. You might like it!

THIRTY-SEVEN

DO THEY GIVE COMPLIMENTS TO OTHERS?

Available are: "Good morning! Great to see you!"

"It is always wonderful to have you here."

"I really appreciate . . . (fill in the blank with anything here) about you" or "I appreciate who you are."

Not to mention all the possible specific things you can find to compliment another person on. Each of these is a Joy booster. Each one raises the vibration of the relationship. As I understand it, the energy of relationships seems to be what the world is made of, therefore, whatever raises the energy vibe of a relationship raises the energy vibe of the world. Sounds good to me. It's like a Joy-making pasta machine. You put in the flour and water; the smile and the compliment, and out come ribbons of Joy. Some people believe, or act as if complimenting another person diminishes them personally, but in reality, people who compliment others are well-anchored in their own ego strength.

One year, my sister, Rachel, said she missed having the Thanksgiving holiday with her sister, me. Dave and I generally drive up north for that holiday. So, I suggested that we have another holiday dinner together and call it "Franksgiving." We could gather and bring hot dogs and sausages and simple side dishes to share. We did this and it was great. I thought that another addition to this holiday, which we plan to keep, a couple weekends before Thanksgiving weekend, would be to tell each other positive, nice things about each other. To add that kind of frankness to the event. It can be a structured way to say the good things that have been left unsaid over the year. Compliments! Try giving ten of these a day and see how your life changes. Call me in the morning.

THIRTY-EIGHT

DO THEY TAKE CARE OF THEIR CLOTHES: SEW ON BUTTONS, FIX HEMS, HANG THINGS UP?

A seamstress? A tailor? Say what? What do buttons and hems have to do with Joy? Am I just too old school? Maybe. My mother and grandmother taught me to do basic hand and machine sewing. It is an endless source of delight, even if I don't get out the machine for months at a time. There is something about being able to make a garment or a piece of cloth functional in a new way or a way it is meant to be. I guess this goes along with "If they see something that is broken, do they fix it?"

Our clothes are sort of an extension of ourselves. They are all full of our skin cells, whether we want to think about that or not, and our movements are what generally make them have a "clothing malfunction." The buttons come off, a hem unravels, we toss them on a chair or on the floor. Well, they cannot fix themselves. Sometimes, they are beyond fixing, and they really do need to be recycled to the ragbag, but many times it is about having a sewing kit and some black thread, some white thread, a needle, and a pair of scissors. Those are the basics. Maybe a couple of straight pins.

Once, I had my mom come to the treatment center where I worked, and with a simple pattern and some cloth and a box of assorted buttons and some small sewing kits, she taught the women there to do those basic sewing tasks by making a cute, stuffed little teddy bear with button eyes.

There is Joy in putting that button back on a shirt so your stomach doesn't hang out, or so that the shirt doesn't have to sit in the closet because the button is not where it is supposed to be. A couple of instructional videos will give more than enough information on how to take care of basic clothes woes. It makes me happy to see each piece function in the way it was meant to function. It adds to the pride and life of the article of clothing, and it adds to me.

Thirty-Nine

DO THEY SEEM TO KNOW THINGS WILL TURN OUT ALL RIGHT?

Some days are diamonds; some days are rust, or is it dust? Anyway, some days are crappy. We have them. We don't like them. My barbell lifting buddy, Lou, told me, "I knew this guy at church. He would do a lot of stuff and you would see him all over the place, but no matter what was happening, he never got ruffled. He was just steady, calm, and contented." So, I figured he was either on some major mood stabilizers, or that he had an inner knowing that things were just going to be okay.

This inner contentment seems to come with a belief that something has got our back. Maybe a Higher Power of some sort. Maybe a sense of karma. Maybe a positive philosophy of life. Maybe just, for us older folks, seeing that the things we were worried about last year are hard to even remember today.

There is Joy in being able to see the positive in most things and in having faith that it all comes out in the wash in the end. I think I just combined two old sayings, but it works for me.

FORTY

DO THEY GIVE
TO CHARITY
CONSISTENTLY?

S haron, my former boss and a wise spiritual teacher who also
happened to run an alcohol and drug abuse treatment center
for women, used to say, "People don't mind giving money for kids
and puppies; it's drunk mothers who are the hard sell." She had a
point. Locally, we have St. Jude Children's Hospital, and, golly, lots
of people donate there. It is a good cause. A very good cause. I am
just hoping, though, that people with Joy in their hearts also look for
the less popular, not-so-flashy places to share their time, talent, and
treasure. Something that pulls on their heartstrings and fires up one
of their passions. I enjoy supporting KIVA, an organization that gives
microloans to small business owners in third world countries. And
there are plenty of places locally and nationally and internationally
that help our marginalized brothers and sisters and nonbinaries to
have a better day.

For gift-giving holidays, I am pretty clear that I do not want or need
any presents. I have more stuff than I can house now. I prefer that
people who want to send something my way donate to a charity or to

a cause of their choice, and I tend to do the same for them. This idea is generally welcomed, and I have seen it spread. So go ahead, spread some Joy!

FORTY-ONE

DO THEY MAKE DIRECT AND KIND EYE CONTACT?

O ur cat, Popcorn, is sitting right next to me on the couch right now. She was my mother's cat. Mom died seven years ago, and Popcorn has continued to live with us. Actually, we moved into mom's house because Popcorn, and her cohort, Lily, were not about to move into the house where we lived across the street. So, we moved in with the cats and eventually sold our house. Seven years later, we still live in Popcorn's house, and she continues to survive. Although an old-lady, buttered-popcorn-colored cat, she is purring and giving me that slow eye blink that I am told means, "I like you," in cat-speak. I look her straight in the eyes and slow blink back at her, hoping that this also means, "I dig you, too, kitty."

But other than with cats, I am not always the best at eye contact, or even face contact. One Thanksgiving, after having been at my sister, Rachel's, home for about an hour, I looked at my brother-in-law, Don. I jumped. He had a nicely grown out white beard to go with his white hair. "Oh, my!" says I. (It looked really good.) He said, "You just noticed? You've been here an hour!" Ah, me. I am not the best at making good, solid direct eye contact. I have to work at it. That was pretty pitiful to not have looked directly at a relative enough to see something that obvious. I'll keep working on it. You do, too.

Forty-Two

DO THEY SEEM TO LIKE THEMSELVES?

D o YOU like yourself? Like, really, really? If you cannot answer that question with a solid yes, then you are not alone in the world. It is amazing how many people really don't. Even some of those people who put on a good act of thinking they've got it all going on and then some, underneath really court self-loathing. There are lots of reasons for this: early messages from caregivers, perceived messages from society, numerous failures or lost opportunities, or sometimes just one or two memorable moments in the past that pierced the heart, broke it, and got stuck there.

Anyway, I am here to tell you that it is all crap. My best therapist advice is to ditch it, pitch it, and don't give it another thought. It's all lies, and you don't need nary a one of them. (If you can do that, bottle it, sell it, and make a mint.) But really, our perceptions as younger people are made through younger eyes, a younger fund of knowledge, and a younger, less sophisticated brain processor. Highly faulty . . . at least for dealing with experiences that were less than nurturing.

Our brains came up with all sorts of ways to survive and try to make sense out of stuff that didn't make much sense. Unfortunately, we believed what we (or someone else) made up and sometimes we still do believe it. A person of Joy has found inner and perhaps outer resources for making adult sense out of all that hooey (giving accountability to whomever really deserves it), has forgiven those misguided or sick folks who didn't know or couldn't or wouldn't do any better, and has moved on. They know that they have a mix of some good stuff and some quirks and faults, and that this is okay. Stewart Smalley told us so, and he was right. "I am good enough, I am smart enough, and darn it, people like me."

Forty-Three

DO THEY APPRECIATE PETS?

N o, they don't have to have a pet. Lots of people don't have pets for very good reasons. But do they appreciate the pets that do cross their paths? There is something about communing with other species that seems to expand who we are. And, perhaps, that happens even more when we get to know a type of animal that we would not have gravitated toward otherwise.

I am not particularly a snake or reptile person, but given some assurances that the pet would be well behaved, I certainly would, and have, spent some time getting acquainted with some non-mainstream sorts of pets.

I was in a pet store in Chicago once and came across some very large tree roaches. I would have to work it up in myself to pal around with one of these, but the proprietor said that they were usually rented out to appear in movies. Remember the one where the roach would carry stuff from one jail cell to another? Yep. That was one of their gigs.

FORTY-FOUR

DO THEY FOLLOW THEIR OWN DRUM BEAT?

I t is not easy to be called outside what seems to be the range of traditional behavior in any particular arena of life. But to have a "call" and to follow it is a powerful thing.

I have a friend, David, who, incidentally, wrote a book entitled "The Call", who was following a planned out educational and career path in science and biology and suddenly had his life trajectory changed by one of those "calls". He has spent his live since then doing inner and outer work to teach, empower and help others and to do his part in healing the planet. I'd be hard-pressed to find anyone with more Joy than I see in him, even in some pretty difficult circumstances.

When we don't follow a calling, there is a depression, self-disappointment, an inner longing that doesn't seem to go away. Often this will get anesthetized away through something intense like drugs, alcohol, food, media-use, or other excitement-laden behaviors or addictions and that makes Joy tricky to find.

So, before judging, see what the path or calling means to that person. You might be surprised what it does to your own insides!

FORTY-FIVE

DO THEY SEE GAMES AND COMPETITION AS FUN RATHER THAN AS WAR?

"We are the Greyhounds, mighty, mighty Greyhounds. Everywhere we go, people want to know, who we are, so we tell them . . . We are the Greyhounds, mighty, mighty Greyhounds. Everywhere we go . . . etc." I remember that from grade school hearing it at Ocean Springs, Mississippi high school football games. Lord only knows why I still remember it. Maybe something about the never-ending loop of words.

Sports and games and activities that are seen as competitive are a conundrum. The various reactions to these events interest me, amaze me, and sometimes piss me off. (Let me rephrase that in good therapist-lingo . . . I get pissed off at it.) I read once in a metaphysical book on history that the early sport games, like the original Olympics, was an intervention from beings out there somewhere, to turn our warlike natures and energies in a different direction so that we would stop killing each other off so rapidly. So that competition could end in a way other than death. Now, that part I like. And maybe the more zealous sport-ball folks who flip over cars and start fights and call the fans and players of the opposing team out-of-their-name (that is Southern talk for calling them mean names) might just still be stuck back in the tribal lets-kill-us-something phase of our development. I am rooting for shaking hands with other athletes in the same sport, saying, "Good game!" and maybe going out for a beer together. Is that a terrible way to think? I think athletes, or game players of any type, who have Joy in their heart can do this, and enjoy the company of people who also enjoy the same activity as they do. Hey, maybe tail-gaiting should happen AFTER the games!

FORTY-SIX

DO THEY HAVE A HOBBY THAT ENGAGES THEM OR SPARKS THEIR CREATIVITY?

"What do you wanna do?" "I don't know, whadaya wanna do?" "I don't know..."

A wild and wonderful therapist under which I trained--Jan was her name--said, "If you're bored, you're boring. Find something to do." I have seen this pretty much play out with folks. Some people want to be entertained and blame others when they are bored, and others find their own entertainment and are never bored.

People with Joy in their heart fit into the second category. There are more possibilities to fill up our time than we could possibly do or even think of. Let's do one alphabet of them...apple picking, bungie jumping, cat petting, dog walking, electronic media, frying donuts, games with friends, hoverboarding--oh, I guess they nixed that one--how about hang-gliding, ice cream kick-the-can (this needs some explaining: you get a can with a lid, a baggie, some salt, some crushed ice, and the makings of a small batch of ice cream. Mix up the ice cream mixture, put it in the small baggie, put that in the can, surrounded with ice and salt, put the lid on, kick it around for about 20 minutes, open the can, pull out the baggie and RINSE off the salt, open it and dish out the ice cream--yum), jumping rope, kick-ball, lamp repair, maker-work (there are studios for that now! Go to one! Have fun!), nuclear physics (learn a bit about it), open a new book, pop some corn, quidditch (the on-the-ground version), rest, silver jewelry-making, tea, underwear sorting (ditch the ones with holes or make rags out of them), vipassana yoga, water some plants, Xena – (check out an episode or two), yard time, zoo. You get the idea.

A really good outcome of this is that when you do enough different things, you actually find ones that you love and that bring you Joy. Cultivate them! People say to work on the things you don't do well so you can get better, but I am thinking that is hooey. Work on the things you like and have some talent for, and have a fabulous time with it!

FORTY-SEVEN

ARE THEY OPEN AND EASY WITHIN THEIR BODY?

O pen body posture: standing up tall (as they are able), arms mobile which move easily out to the sides and front, feet slightly apart with even weight. Quick to hug or touch another when appropriate. Not hunching in on oneself. When you have Joy in your heart, you don't feel you have to defend yourself against everything. You basically know the world is there for you. You are usually comfortable in your skin and easy in your body. And it shows. I think I feel this about half of the time. Maybe I can claim half-Joy on this one.

I try using the "power" positions. About two minutes of one of these can help with a feeling of confidence:

1. The Wonder Woman or Superman position: fists on hips, feet apart, standing tall.

2. The Victorious Runner position: both arms and hands in the air. Try this in private before going into a scary situation like a job interview.

3. The Power Lean: standing, lean forward onto a table with

hands on the table.

4. The Expanded Body Space position; put your arm across the chair next to you.

5. Feet on the Desk position: this is a bit arrogant but gives off the impression of confidence if you don't dump the chair. Don't dump the chair.

What all this has to do with Joy, I am not sure, but I did want to share those little confidence builders with you. Oh, and you don't need the cape.

FORTY-EIGHT

DO THEY STILL DO SOME FUN THINGS THEY LIKED AS A CHILD?

Maybe it is swinging on a swing, or non-serious swimming in a pool (laps don't count), camping or licking mixing bowl beaters (lets not talk about the raw egg thing), coloring or playing with clay, basketball or pulling apart sandwich cookies and eating the frosting, or getting their fingers really orange from cheese snacks, or throwing a Frisbee or ball, or rolling around with a dog. Perhaps it is singing songs they have known since childhood, or listening to stories, or walking around in pajamas.

What fun things do you still do that you did as a child?

FORTY-NINE

DO THEY TAKE THEIR TURN DOING SOMETHING UNPLEASANT, LIKE CHORES?

Some chores are not pleasant. Even the word *chore* tends to make us groan. Does anyone else get a reaction from the phrase "you're not the boss of me" like I do? My inner rebellious child comes out and I do not want to do many things I feel like I have to do. I don't wanna!

Chores are about maintenance of our stuff or maybe the stuff we share with others. Interestingly, there is great variety in what we each are okay with doing and with what we really don't like. My Aunt Judy once said that she really liked putting her house in order and doing chores, and that was the first time I had heard that from anyone. She liked to putter, and it showed. She had a million things, but they each had their place. So, with chores it is more like different strokes for different folks. Some people really like doing chores I might find reprehensible and vice versa. But there are some things that are just not intrinsically fun for most folks, and a person with Joy in their heart knows that and will take a turn, by golly! Often without being asked. And won't whine about it. Nothing lasts forever.

FIFTY

DO THEY HANG AROUND OTHER PEOPLE WITH JOY IN THEIR HEART?

"You can tell the character of a person by the company they keep."
"If you sleep with dogs you're gonna get fleas."
"Change your people, places and things."

You know the sayings. Not only are we judged by the company we keep; we are influenced by them. Often people who do not feel great about themselves will surround themselves with people that are in a worse situation. This can serve to make them feel better than those other people. There is some reward in feeling like top dog, even if in a very small kennel. People with Joy in their heart generally have a mix of people with whom they associate. There will be some to whom they go to for assistance, some whom they help, and some who are at about the same peer level. They often have someone they look up to who helps them move forward and possibly listens to them process whatever comes at them day to day. They have people they can trust and often they have people who trust them. They don't tend to judge others, so they can make friends from many walks of life.

Joy is what we feel when sharing love. "Love" is giving out the very best that we have, that we know. It is a powerful expression of healing. It may be found in a rose, in a child's smile, in music, in friendship, in acts of service to others, in working with the hands, in kindness, in serving a Higher Power. It is being our Soul's expression on Earth in whatever way It chooses to express. Doing that with others is an excellent way to experience Joy.

IN CONCLUSION

I hope you have found this book to be interesting, informative and maybe a little bit inspiring. I think I have inspired myself by listening to friends talk about their ideas about how to tell if someone has Joy in their heart. I thank them all for their input.

Whether you are looking for a friend, friendly co-worker, person to have coffee with, or to date, perhaps having a way to assess whether they have Joy in their heart might be helpful. Maybe it will curtail some drama or trauma down the road. Or, maybe trying out some of these ideas might help create a little more Joy in your own ticker. Hey! Anything is possible! Thanks for listening.

— Elaine Orland

THE CHECKLIST

nswer the best you can. With some of these items, you might think, "Sometimes yes, sometimes no." With those, you will have to decide which is the more consistent answer.

Do They have Joy in Their Heart – A Checklist

- Yes No **1 Do they wake up happy in the morning?**

- Yes No **2 Do they use turn signals when other cars are in sight?**

- Yes No **3 Do they speak well of past relationships?**

- Yes No **4 Do they tip generously in restaurants?**

- Yes No **5 Do they have a spirituality that they practice that brings them peace?**

- Yes No **6 Do they have a guiding ideal?**

- Yes No **7 When they see something that is wrong or broken, do they try to fix it rather than ignore it or pass** it on to someone else?

- Yes No **8 Do they have a sense of humor?**

- Yes No **9 Do they easily help set things up and clean up afterward?**

- Yes No **10 Do they not take things personally, realizing that everything is not about them?**

- Yes No **11 Are they easy to approach for assistance or in general?**

- Yes No **12 Can they laugh at themselves?**

- Yes No **13 Do they help out without being asked?**

- Yes No **14 Do they find the positive in any situation?**

- Yes No **15 Do they listen carefully?**

- Yes No **16 Can they admit when they are wrong?**

- Yes No **17 Do they let other drivers merge in front of them?**

- Yes No **18 Do they enjoy being around children?**

- Yes No **19 Do they reach out to family and friends and keep in touch?**

- Yes No **20 Do they keep the front walk or entryway swept?**

- Yes No **21 Do they experience wonder in the natural**

world?

- Yes No **22 If they are making something, do they make extra for others...or at least share?**

- Yes No **23 If they have an addiction, are they in a solid recovery lifestyle?**

- Yes No **24 Are they kind to wait staff and persons with service jobs?**

- Yes No **25 Are they content with what they have?**

- Yes No **26 Do they make their bed when they get up?**

- Yes No **27 Do they return the shopping cart to the store or official cart parking place?**

- Yes No **28 Do they forgive easily?**

- Yes No **29 Do they send thank you notes or thoughtful messages?**

- Yes No **30 Do they laugh easily?**

- Yes No **31 Do they try to understand and encourage others and never tear them down?**

- Yes No **32 Do they smile through their eyes?**

- Yes No **33 Are they patient and compassionate when that is called for?**

- Yes No **34 Do they sing, whistle, hum, or dance regularly?**

- Yes No **35 Do they volunteer some of their time?**

- Yes No **36 Do they say "I love you" to friends?**

- Yes No **37 Do they give compliments to others?**

- Yes No **38 Do they take care of their clothes: sew on buttons, fix hems, hang things up?**

- Yes No **39 Do they seem to know things will turn out all right?**

- Yes No **40 Do they give to charity consistently?**

- Yes No **41 Do they make direct and kind eye contact?**

- Yes No **42 Do they seem to like themselves?**

- Yes No **43 Do they appreciate pets?**

- Yes No **44 Do they follow their own drum beat?**

- Yes No **45 Do they see games and competition as fun rather than as war?**

- Yes No **46 Do they have a hobby that engages them or sparks their creativity?**

- Yes No **47 Are they open and easy within their body?**

- Yes No **48 Do they still do some fun things they liked as a child?**

- Yes No **49 Do they take their turn doing something unpleasant, like chores?**

- Yes No **50 Do they hang around other people with Joy in their heart?**

___ **Total Marked "Yes"**

Scoring:

Count the items circled "Yes."

- 1-5—They need some lightening up. Take care around them. Maybe play it safe and run away.

- 6-20—They have some Joy trying to work up and out.

- 21-30—They are well on their way.

- 31-40—They have some real joy in their heart (or maybe anxiety, if our daughter has anything to say about it.)

- 41-50—You are probably fooling yourself or too much in love already to see clearly.

ABOUT AUTHOR

Elaine Orland is a social worker and therapist surrounded by wise and wonderful people. She lives in Tennessee in an extended family home full of family and pets. Her family publishing business usually produces other people's work, but this was one of those little books that just needed to happen.

Made in United States
Troutdale, OR
02/02/2024

17224803R00065